101 WAYS TO IMPROVE YOUR
Knitting

SUSAN BATES PRESENTS

101 WAYS TO IMPROVE YOUR
Knitting

by Barbara Abbey

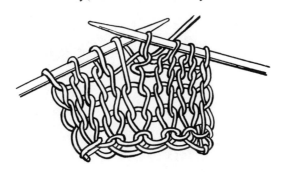

A Studio Book

The Viking Press • New York

CONTENTS

INTRODUCING ... MISS BARBARA ABBEY

Barbara Abbey learned to knit when she was three years old by following illustrations in a picture book. Her needles were two pencils and her yarn was a piece of string. She recalls too that her first long chain of crocheting was accomplished by means of an old-fashioned shoe-buttonhook. She was always busy in one way or another with fancy work, through the "violets and daisies on pillow-tops" stage, on to filet netting and tatted laces with No. 150 thread.

She planned a concert career, and the violin and viola were the preoccupations of her school-age days. Later, after completing the five-year course in four years, she received her degree of Bachelor of Music at Yale University. She concentrated on composition there and used the prizes awarded her to further her music studies in Vienna. She played in symphony orchestras for eleven years and, during this time, did some concert work in singing as well as violin.

However, her hobby of needlework began to occupy more and more of her time, encroaching on her musical activities to the point that *they* became her hobby and knitting and designing her profession. The more satisfying experience of working out complicated patterns in various types of handwork—bobbin laces, petit and gros point, thread laces, embroideries—progressed to designing and teaching at the nationally known needlework headquarters, Alice Maynard, Inc., in New York City. She now has her own knitting studio in Pell Lake, Wisconsin, and each day new problems are presented by customers, for which solutions must be found.

Through contact and association with literally thousands of people who knit as a hobby, the very real need for a book on this subject became apparent to her. For those who start to knit, the mere act of learning how to use needles and yarn is only the beginning. *Then* arise the problems which every knitter will sooner or later have to face.

Barbara Abbey actually *likes* to teach and, as she was daily presented with certain problems, she adopted the habit of writing down the answers to them. These problems and their solutions are what led her to write this very practical little volume. We are proud to present it to you, for we know just how helpful you will find it.

SUSAN BATES
C. J. Bates & Son, Inc.
Chester, Connecticut

FOREWORD

This is not an instruction book, nor is it written to teach the fundamental steps of using needles and yarn to make a piece of knitted material. Its sole purpose is to help the knitter avoid the numerous little traps which lie in her path, to make her more independent of the instructor, *and also* to make the written instructions in knitting books easier to understand and interpret. Keep it in your knitting bag for handy reference.

Many changes in types of yarns and new equipment are being constantly developed, but the following suggestions remain valid and will generally apply to problems that may arise. They have been compiled in the course of answering questions that were presented repeatedly and demanded logical solutions. When the knitter understands *why* certain procedures are followed, the problems cease to exist.

It should be understood that many procedures outlined in this book are not easy. Any unfamiliar method requires patience and practice, but, in time, the ultimate of personal satisfaction *can* be obtained.

It may seem to the reader that certain words and phrases have been repeated excessively in the following pages. This repetition is intentional, and for one reason: emphasis and re-emphasis upon the methods given, plus the possible help of a good instructor, are the sure way to keep the knitter in the path of good knitting habits. These methods make knitting instructions more intelligible and eliminate the necessity of losing valuable time in duplication of work and effort.

BARBARA ABBEY

101 WAYS TO IMPROVE YOUR KNITTING

EQUIPMENT

(1)   Knitting is a form of expression. Not everyone can be an artist, writer, or composer, but if you can take yarn and fashion from it an article that is serviceable and attractive, you have created a masterpiece of practical art.

Knitting requires very little equipment for any one article, but it must be the best if you are to attain the greatest enjoyment and relaxation from your endeavor—although good equipment alone will not automatically result in perfect work. If your knitting needles are heavy, too rigid, or too pliable, with blunt points that split the yarn, or sharp points that hurt the fingers, knitting becomes a chore, and the finished work will reflect this. To be sure of avoiding any of these difficulties, it is advisable to get *precision-tapered* knitting needles, the points of which are designed to slide easily through the stitches without splitting the yarn. They also have good balance, are light in weight, and are sufficiently flexible to permit long hours of work without tiring the hands and shoulders.

These needles are available in various materials to allow you to choose the type you prefer for the work planned. If you wish a firm needle there is, for instance, the *Silvalume* (special aluminum alloy) precision-tapered needle with a smooth permanent finish that does not soil light-colored yarns. The more flexible needle is made of *Luxite,* a plastic-like material with greater strength and durability than most, while *Tonewood* is a highly polished hard wood, in which precision-tapered needles are available in larger sizes only, for ribbons or very bulky yarns, or for a loose mesh effect.

Knitting needles are made in single-point, double-point, or circular types. Single-point needles are sometimes referred to as STRAIGHT needles and are used for any back-and-forth knitting. Double-point needles, often referred to as SOCK needles for obvious reasons, are also recommended for many knitted pieces where seams would detract from appearance and fit; also for neckline finishes and many other purposes.

Circular knitting needles are used for many different types of work. The shorter lengths (9, 11, 16 inches) may be used for sleeves, round-neck ribbing, small garments, etc. The longer lengths (24 to 29 inches) are used in making sweaters, coats, skirts, and dresses.

The smaller sizes (generally from size 0 through size 5) have working tips of rustproof metal; the connecting portion is of strong, flexible Dupont nylon that will not break or fray; the joints are smooth and will not catch the yarn. Larger sizes, from size 6 through size 10½, are of all-nylon construction.

SIZES AND LENGTHS AVAILABLE IN KNITTING NEEDLES

| | SINGLE POINTS | | DOUBLE POINTS | |
MATERIALS	LENGTHS	SIZES	LENGTHS	SIZES
Aluminum Type (Silvalume*)	7–inch	0–5	5–inch	0–3
	10–inch	0–15	7 & 10–inch	0–8
	12–inch	0–8		
	14–inch	0–15		
Plastic Type (Luxite*)	10 & 14–inch	1–15	7–inch	1–8
Wood (Tonewood*)	14–inch	10–11	Not available	
		13–15		

| CIRCULAR NEEDLES | |
LENGTHS	SIZES
9–inch	1–3
11–inch	0–3
16–inch	0–8
24–inch	0–10
29–inch	0–10½

(*Special materials in which precision-tapered needles are made.)

Whether or not you crochet, knitting equipment is not complete without a few crochet hooks. They are necessary for finishing a knitted garment and for picking up "lost" stitches. Many people have trouble with crochet hooks that too easily allow the stitches to slip off and also tend to split the yarn. There is a wonderfully designed hook made by Susan Bates which may well prove a boon to you if you haven't already tried it. The hook is well defined to avoid splitting threads. Also, the head of the hook is in line with the shaft, which prevents the stitches from slipping off and keeps the stitches at the same working gauge, assuring smoother operation. The steel sizes come in regular finish at the top. They are also made, however, with a clip at the top end to allow the worker to slip the stitch under this clip when work is interrupted.

The following sizes and types of hooks are helpful when the knitter is finishing her work. As this is a *knitting* guide, not all sizes of hooks are presented here,

MATERIALS	SIZES	WEIGHT OF YARNS USED IN KNITTING
Steel	3–7	Lightweight yarns; bouclé, nubby yarns
Bone	1–2	2- and 3-ply fingering and baby wools
	3–4	3-ply fingering and baby wools
	5–6	Knitting Worsted, Sport Yarns, or double strands of lightweight yarns
Aluminum Type (Silvalume) and	B/1–C/2	2- and 3-ply fingering yarns and baby wools
Plastic Type (Luxite)	D/3–E/4–F/5 G/6–H/8–I/9 J/10–K/10½	Heavy-weight yarns or double strands of medium-weight yarns; all bulky yarns; ribbons

The following knitting aids have been purposely designed to make easier the little tasks necessary to the working, finishing, and proper fit of garments.

Yarneedle. To sew the seams of knitted garments and for wool embroidery.

Knit Count. By twisting the little dials, you can easily keep count of rows as you make them.

Stitch Holders. To hold stitches securely when not in use. These are available in aluminum and plastic materials; in small, medium, and large sizes. Also available are the *Midget Stitch Holders,* which are ideal for holding a very small number of stitches.

Cablestitch Holder. The curve holds the stitches securely, making cablestitching easier. Use the holder in all cases when instructions call for a spare needle. The size is just right for all types of yarn, regardless of the size of knitting needle used.

Yarn Bobbins. For multi-color knitting and argyle socks. These are made in various sizes and shapes. They allow the yarn to unwind smoothly and evenly; lock and unlock the yarn as wanted; prevent knots and tangles; hold generous quantities of yarn.

Ring Markers. To slip onto the needle to mark work into designated sections for increases or decreases, etc. Invaluable when making skirts or sweaters where counting of stitches is difficult.

Knit Chek. Designed to check stitch and row gauge more easily and accurately. For details on the proper way to check *your* gauge, see Tip 22 and Figures 1 and 2. The importance of doing this cannot be overemphasized.

Fig. 1

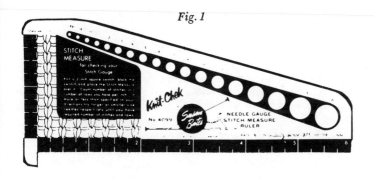

Fig. 2

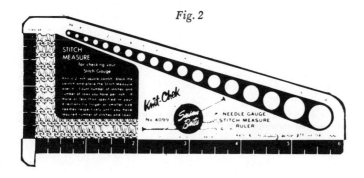

For best results, measure size of your knitting needles and crochet hooks (except steel hooks) with this same Knit Chek, which shows the accurate *standard* sizes called for in most instructions.

(2) It is wise to include the following items of equipment, although they are not usually thought of before an emergency arises:

> Tape Measure
> Scissors (kept in a case for safety)
> Transparent 6-inch ruler
> Nail file and emery board (for catchy fingernails)
> Blunt-pointed tapestry needles
> Notebook and pencil
> Small transparent case to keep all easily lost items within easy reach

HINTS ON EQUIPMENT

(3) Properly nickel-plated needles should not rust but, if your equipment is old, keep steel needles and hooks from rusting by putting them in a long, stoppered bottle with a small piece of camphor wrapped in cloth.

(4) Wooden needles may develop rough and catchy spots. To remedy this, dip a very slightly dampened cloth in a fine-grain kitchen cleanser and rub the needle with this. Let dry thoroughly, then rub off all the dry cleanser with a rough cloth and polish by rubbing hard with a thick fold of heavy waxed paper.

(5) Tender fingers are apt to get sore when working on harsh or knotty yarn. Cut the finger from an old kid glove and slip it over the offended finger.

(6) When going to a shop for knitting instructions, put a small notebook in your knitting bag. Listen carefully for all suggestions made by your instructor to *anyone,* not just to yourself, and make notes of them. Read these notes carefully when you get home and write them—in your own words—in a permanent notebook; or write them in the back pages of this book, which were left blank for just this purpose. These notes may prove invaluable later.

YARNS

There are literally hundreds of different kinds and textures of yarns   (7)
made available by manufacturers. They are spun from practically all
kinds of natural fibers, which include silk, cotton, linen, wool, and
hair fibers (mohair, cashmere, angora, alpaca, vicuña, etc.) synthetics
of all kinds (and new ones constantly in the process of development),
and various combinations of all of the foregoing. They may be fine
and loosely twisted to produce soft, fluffy articles, or tightly twisted
to give a hard, smooth, long-wearing quality. Some are crinkly, giving
a crepy finish; others are interspersed with small knots, large fluffy
knots, or metallic knots. Some are heavy and either smooth and soft
or rough and woolly. Others are tightly twisted with shiny fibers or
metallic threads worked into them for the making of dressy clothes
for daytime or evening wear. There are mixtures of different colors
which are perfect for tweed fabric effects. There are fat, lightweight
"bulky" yarns for sweaters, coats, and dresses which are so popular in
high fashion. All these yarns have their own distinct places in the
scheme of knitting and have been spun and dyed in a great variety
of textures and shades of colors to give the knitter an almost unlimited
choice.

Ribbons for hand-knitting must certainly be included here. They
are used principally for dresses, blouses, suits, etc., and are knitted
either alone or in combination with yarns of all descriptions. The
widths commonly found are 3/16 inch and 1/4 inch, and the materials
used in their manufacture are usually rayon or silk or various combinations of these. The textures range from the heavier thicknesses
down through the very finest, almost transparent organdies. Some of
these organdy ribbons have metallic threads woven into them for
dressy "after-five" clothes. Also, many of the heavier types of materials,
either soft-textured or crisp taffeta-textured, are woven with two or
more colors to produce "tweed" effects. All these ribbons have their
own special uses to produce the desired results.

Today we no longer think of knitting in terms of socks, sweaters,
or purely utility garments. Because of the great new developments and
improvements in materials, and also because designing and styling
have advanced to such a high degree, knitted clothes are not just
acceptable; they are highly desirable in every woman's wardrobe.
They are practically indispensable for the traveler.

Because of the constant change in weights and types of yarns and
ribbons, there is no need for a chart to indicate sizes of needles to be

used for the various items which can be made. The determining factor in making *any* garment or article is the GAUGE called for in the instructions. Read *very carefully* the directions in Tips 21 through 25, and then apply these suggestions to the written instructions given for the article or garment you wish to make. The very first thing to look for in *any* instruction is the GAUGE. This is most commonly found at the very beginning of the article written about the particular item to be worked, and included with the type of yarn, size or sizes of needle or needles to be used, etc. This insistence on GAUGE *cannot possibly be stressed too strongly.*

HINTS ON YARNS

(8)   *Always* buy sufficient yarn to make the complete garment. In most brands, no two dye lots are *exactly* the same, and an unsightly streak in the garment, because more than one dye lot has been used, can prove to be a real tragedy. Before leaving the shop, be sure that all packages are checked for the *color number and the dye-lot marking,* to see that they are the same.

If there is doubt about the amount of yarn to purchase, it is far better to buy *more* than less. Many shops will be glad to refund the purchase price on the unused, unbroken skeins or balls if they are kept in good condition and have not been kept too long a time after the date of purchase. Keep all wrappers or identifying marks and purchase receipts until garment is completed. It is a very good idea to write pertinent information about each article you knit in your notebook: date purchased, dye-lot number, color number, and amount purchased.

(9)   When choosing yarn, remember that there is less yardage per ounce in crinkly or nubby types than in those of smooth, light texture such as cashmere or fine two-ply yarn. In making a garment, therefore, you will have to count on using more ounces of the former kind of yarn than the latter.

(10)   When a knitted woolen garment, such as a bathing suit, is to be worn in the water, it is advisable to use a double strand of lightweight yarn (three- or four-ply fingering) worked on a smaller needle rather than a single strand of heavier weight yarn. Here again, check the GAUGE to make certain it is correct. There is more stretch and drag when the

garment is wet. Use two balls of yarn and work the two together. Where colors can be matched, it is highly desirable to have one of the strands of nylon, or nylon and yarn mixture. This combination of wool and nylon fibers will give the added advantage of warmth plus quick drying. *Always use a color-fast yarn.*

When making a ball from a hank, always wind yarn *loosely*. If yarn (11) is wound tightly, the life and stretch are seriously impaired. Wind around the fingers and thumb of one hand, and continue to do this throughout the winding of the whole hank.

When using any light-colored yarn that comes already wound, use (12) from the *outside* of the ball, as dust inevitably collects on the outside when ball is in use, thus making a soiled streak through otherwise clean work. Also, yarn and work may be kept in a cloth or plastic bag when not in use.

Don't be timid about working with brands or textures of yarns dif- (13) ferent from those called for in the instruction books. In pattern or fabric stitches, it isn't at all necessary to stick to the regulation types of yarns or colors specified. The possibilities are limitless as regards stitches, color combinations, and texture effects. Good taste, good measurements (Tip 20) and GAUGE (again) are the important regulating factors. So play around with colors and types of yarns. It is a fascinating diversion which may lead to lovely and original effects.

To Re-Use Yarn: Rip out all yarn and wind into skeins on a large (14) book or box or some similar object. Be sure to keep the starting end visible, then slip off and tie the end of yarn to the starting end. Then, with other small pieces, tie *loosely* in four places. Wash and rinse thoroughly. Press out all water possible, then put in an absorbent towel and wring. Hang in a dry place. If yarn is still wrinkled from the previous knitting, tie a small weight to the bottom of hank while drying.

ABBREVIATIONS

The following abbreviations of knitting terms appear in most instruc- (15) tion sheets, and many of them are also used in this book.

K	—Knit
P	—Purl
St (s)	—Stitch (es)
tog.	—together
Sl	—Slip
yo (O)	—yarn over the needle
SKP; Sl, K and psso; or Slip, knit and pass	—Slip 1 st, K 1 st and pass the slipped st over the knit st
dec.	—decrease
inc.	—increase
beg.	—beginning
rnd.	—round (in circular knitting or when using DP needles)
DP (dp)	—double-pointed (needles)
rep. or rpt.	—repeat
work even	—continue to work as you have been doing, without increasing or decreasing
Sl st	—slip-stitch (in crochet)
sc	—single crochet (in crochet)
"	—inch

(16) *In reading instructions from a book,* when an asterisk (*) appears, you will invariably find another (*) in the same sentence. This means that something is to be repeated in the row of work which that sentence describes. You should repeat only those sts which appear *between* the two asterisks, not the sts which are written before or after them. As an example, in the following row of a pattern stitch you find:

P 1, * P 1, K 2, P 1, K 4; rep. from *, ending row with P 1, K 2, P 2.

You should work the *first* P 1 *one time only* to begin with, *then* P 1, K 2, P 1, K 4, and repeat just this P 1, K 2, P 1, K 4 to the end of the row, where you will find that you have only five sts remaining. These five sts are not enough to work between the two * *, which would take eight sts. Therefore, work the sts that come *after* the last *, which are P 1, K 2, P 2.

(17) *Pattern stitches are always worked with a definite multiple of stitches.* Count the number of sts between the two * * as your *multiple,* then add the extra sts before and after these * * together for *additional* sts. For example, if your pattern stitch reads as in Tip 16, your multiple of sts would be eight plus six. You should count the eight sts between the two * * for the *multiple* and the one purled st before the first * and the five sts after the last * as your *additional* sts. See also Tip 38.

STANDARD SIZES

To help you determine what size garment to make, the Standard *Body* (18)
Measurements listed below are those which are designated in leading
knitting books, *not* pattern books. These sizes do not in any way
correspond to the size slip, dress, or bra you wear. They are only a
guide to help you choose the size of *knitted* garment you wish to make.

	SIZE	CHEST	WAIST	HIPS	ARM-HOLE	SLEEVE LENGTH
Infants & Children	9 mo.	19			3¼	6
	1 yr.	20			3¾	7
	2	21			4	8
	3	22	20½	23	4¼	8¼
	4	23	21	24	4½	8½
	5	23½	21½	25	5	10
	6	24	22	26	5½	11
	8	26	23	29	6	12
	10	28	24	30	6½	14
		BUST				
Misses & Women	10	31	24	33	7¼	16¼
	12	32	25	34	7½	17
	14	34	26	36	7¾	17
	16	36	28	38	8	17½
	18	38	30	40	8½	18
	20	38–40	32	42	9	18
		CHEST				
Men	36	36	33		8	20
	38	38	34		8¼	20
	40	40	36		8½	21
	42	42	38		9	21
	44	44	40		9½	21½

In all the foregoing references, to repeat, it *must* be remembered that (19)
the measurements are *standard measurements only,* and that they may
not necessarily apply to *your* figure. For instance, you may have the
same bust measurement as indicated in any size on the chart, but your
waist, hips, or armhole all may differ considerably from those in that
same size. For the proper fit of *your* garment, you must take *your*
measurements carefully and plan all work to coincide with them.

HOW TO TAKE MEASUREMENTS

(20)   *Bust Measurement* (women). Around the fullest part of bust, holding tape measure up slightly at the back.

Chest Measurement (men and children). Around the fullest part of chest, with chest fully expanded.

Underarm to Waist. From the underarm at seam, not at very pit of arm, but about one inch down from the pit of arm, to exact waistline.

Shoulder to Waist in Front. From exact top of shoulder across fullest part of bust to the exact waistline. This will be a slightly diagonal line.

Neck to Waist in Back. From "dowager's hump" at back of neck to center of exact waistline.

Shoulder to Shoulder in Back. From top of shoulder-bone on one side to same point on other side.

Neck to Shoulder. From side of neck to top of shoulder-bone.

Armhole. From top of shoulder *straight* down to one inch below pit of arm. Measure this straight down; *do not curve in.*

Sleeve Length. Measure from about 1 inch from pit of arm straight down inside of arm to wrist bone. This is for long sleeve only. Other desired lengths should be measured accordingly.

Arm. Top arm, forearm, wrist. Take exact measurement of largest part of each.

Hip. Measure the *very fullest part of the seat* found below the waistline. Also, mark this point and measure down from the exact waistline to this point, at side.

Length of Skirt. Measure length of skirt from exact waistline, down the side, to the exact desired length. For a large figure, it is important that two measurements be taken—from waistline at front to bottom edge, and from waistline at back as well.

It is a rare coincidence to find two sets of measurements which exactly match. Most of the differences lie in the measurements from underarm to waist (long-waisted or short-waisted), and the measurement of the hip around and down from waist. Give great attention to each of these measurements, therefore.

HOW TO DETERMINE YOUR GAUGE

CORRECT GAUGE IS THE MOST IMPORTANT FACTOR IN THE FIT OF ANY KNITTED OR CROCHETED GARMENT.

To Make Swatch. When using a simple stitch such as **Garter**, **Stock-**   (21)
inette, or seed stitch in the body (or main part) of the garment, cast
on about 24 sts, *using the very same yarn and color* you will use, and
the size needles indicated in the directions. Work about 3 inches and
remove from needle without binding off.

After removing the swatch from the needles, flatten it out as it natu-   (22)
rally would lie, on a hard flat surface. Observe carefully that each
stitch is made up of two threads forming a loop. When counting
stitches, do not count every little hole as a stitch; count one *loop* as
a stitch.

Place a small ruler or your Knit Chek over the swatch (Fig. 1)
and count the number of sts in *two full inches.* Divide this number
in half and you have *your* stitch gauge for one inch. For example,
if you count 15 sts in two inches, your gauge will be 7½ sts to the inch;
16 sts will be a gauge of 8 sts to the inch, and so on. DO NOT
UNDERESTIMATE THE IMPORTANCE OF HALF A STITCH
IN AN INCH. In the over-all measurement, this *half-stitch* will make
a considerable difference in the total number of stitches required.

*Never use a pliable measure or hold swatch in hands to measure
gauge.* Also, and this is most important, NEVER WORK A SWATCH
FOR ANOTHER PERSON NOR LET ANOTHER PERSON
WORK YOUR SWATCH.

When estimating gauge, count the number of rows in an inch as   (23)
well as the number of sts. Turn work over to the purled (or wrong)
side (Fig. 2) and count the ridges, particularly in Stockinette Stitch.
This wrong-side counting of rows is also useful when exact numbers
of rows must be determined in a pattern, or in counting the number
of rows during the working of an article.

Do not use *any* pattern stitch as an authentic gauge for any *other*   (24)
pattern stitch. Do not use *any* pattern stitch as a gauge for Stockinette
Stitch. *All* pattern stitches can differ to a marked degree. In other
words, when using *any* pattern stitch, regardless of what it is, take
your gauge in *that stitch* which is to be used in the main part of the
piece you are making. *This is most important.* If more than one type
of pattern stitch is to be used, *take both gauges.*

When you plan to knit in an open lacy pattern, it is advisable to   (25)
make a six-inch square of the pattern stitch and block it to the fullest
extent of stretch before determining gauge *per rows* as well as stitches
to the inch. When measuring the over-all distance in this kind of work,

make sure to take the amount of stretch into consideration when computing the length of the piece.

(26) When you find that you have too *few* sts in an inch, your work is too loose. Use a smaller size needle to acquire the correct gauge. If you have too *many* sts in an inch, your work is too tight. Use a larger needle to get the correct gauge. Again, do not let another person work a swatch for you. *You* must make it for yourself. It is perfectly possible for four people to make four completely different gauges with the exact same yarn and needles.

(27) There are many cases where a knitter will find a marked dissimilarity in tension between the knitted and purled rows. Of course, it is firmly advised to seek a means of overcoming this difficulty, if possible. If not, however, try using two sizes of needles, the smaller needle for the looser row and the larger needle for the tighter row.

(28) Another color of the same type of yarn is very apt to make a change in gauge. The dye used can cause a decided change in the thickness of the yarn, enough to make a complete difference in the size of the garment. Therefore, if you have made a white blouse which you like very much and which fits you to perfection, do *not* attempt to make it in another color until you have made your gauge in that same color.

(29) Keep a constant watch on your tension during the working of any garment. Check your gauge every few inches, particularly when work has been interrupted for any length of time. *Even the way you feel* may make a difference. Worry, illness, or irritation of any kind will almost invariably tighten your gauge, while happiness and relaxation will have the opposite effect.

CASTING ON

(30) *Casting On with One Needle.* Leave about a yard and a half for each hundred sts when fine yarn is used—more for heavier yarns. Hold thread in two back fingers of both hands (Fig. 3), the shorter end in the left hand. With right hand, draw thread *under* the left thumb *toward* you, and then *away* from you *over* the thumb (Fig. 4). Then, using the index finger of the left hand as a hook, lay finger on *top* of yarn and hook the finger toward the crotch of the thumb and forefinger; then straighten this finger up (Fig. 5). Use the resulting loop on the finger as a stitch, insert the needle into the *front* of this loop (Fig. 6), and use the thread in the right hand for knitting this stitch onto the right-hand needle. Continue this procedure for the

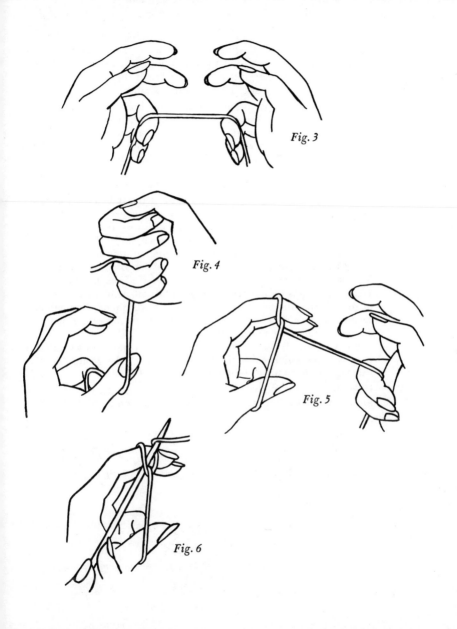

Fig. 3

Fig. 4

Fig. 5

Fig. 6

desired number of sts. Casting on in this manner is a slight deviation from the usual one-needle method. However, the extra cross-twist in the loop on the finger gives a resulting firmer, but not tighter, edge at beginning of the work. This is most desirable.

(31) *Casting On with Two Needles.* Put a slip knot onto the left-hand needle (Fig. 7). Holding the yarn in the right hand, knit into the stitch with the second needle and pull the loop through, but do not remove the original loop from the left-hand needle. Put the loop that you pulled through, back onto the left-hand needle, twisting the right-hand needle so that, when you slip this loop on, the two needle-points are facing in the same direction (Fig. 8). From this point on, instead of knitting into this second stitch on the left-hand needle, as is the ordinary practice, insert the needle-point *in between* the two stitches on the needle (Fig. 9), wrap yarn, and pull this loop through from *between* the stitches, not through the stitch itself. Twist this loop back onto the left-hand needle. Continue in this manner for the desired number of sts. This method of casting on sts gives a firmer, less loopy edge, more like that of the preferred one-needle method. When directions indicate the addition of numbers of sts at beginning of rows during the progress of work, the above two-needle method of casting on should be used. This does not mean *increasing,* it means adding more than one st at any given point.

You will find that when you work back on the next row an unsightly loop will present itself at the first cast-on st of the group. To close this hole, either knit or purl into the *back* of this st.

(32) If you find that you have a tendency to cast on too tightly, or bind off too tightly, use a larger size needle for the cast-on or bind-off row.

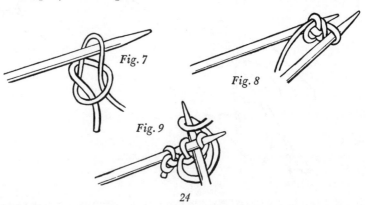

Fig. 7

Fig. 8

Fig. 9

WORKING OF THE KNITTED PIECE

In nearly every written instruction, you will find at one point or (33) another a direction involving numbers of rows. Simply keep in mind that every time you work the sts from one needle onto the other needle, this constitutes the making of one row, regardless of whether this row comes on the right or wrong side of the work.

One of the best knitted pieces for a beginner to make is a V-neck (34) sweater, for practically all the problems that arise in knitting will at one time or another have to be solved during its making. On the other hand, a scarf or other such very simple article is dull, tedious work and provides little incentive for learning. Making an article which can be worn with pride inspires you to go ahead.

For a better seam in K 2, P 2 ribbing, read your instructions for the (35) number of cast-on sts. If they are divisible by *four,* cast on two sts *less* than the given amount in the directions; then work as follows:

Row 1: * K 2, P 2, K 2, P 2—rep. from * across the row, ending row with K 2.

Row 2: * P 2, K 2, P 2, K 2—rep. from * across the row, ending row with P 2.

Repeat these two rows for the desired amount of ribbing and, when working the last row, increase one st at each end of the needle. You will find, when joining seams, that the ribbing at the edge of the seam will form a complete pattern in ribbing.

For K 1, P 1 ribbing, substitute K 1, P 1 for the K 2, P 2, using an uneven number of sts, or one less than called for if an even number is indicated in the instructions. Make up the extra st on the last row of ribbing. More and more instruction books are adopting this more satisfactory method of ribbing.

Tighter Ribbing. Instead of the customary K 1, P 1 or K 2, P 2 ribbing (36) at bottoms of sweaters, sleeves, or such, work your ribbing for four rows as usual. Then, for K 1, P 1 ribbing, substitute K 1, Sl 1 for the usual K 1, P 1 on the first row, and purl all sts on the return row. This may be done when a tighter border is desired. This ribbing allows for less stretch and holds more firmly. However, when using this method of ribbing at the bottom edge of a knitted piece, it is wiser to work four to six rows on a smaller needle in the regular method of ribbing, as the slipped ribbing has a tendency to curl outward which is not desirable. This slipped ribbing is particularly good for taking in fullness abruptly, such as ribbing at waistlines or yokes.

(37)   *Cross-Stitch Ribbing.* A delicate and very effective variation of ribbing is this cross-stitch ribbing. It can be used anywhere on any sweater where ribbing is indicated. Cast on a multiple of 3 sts plus 1—13, 25, 34, 40, etc.—and proceed as follows:

     Row 1: * P 1, skip 1 st and K the 2nd st on left-hand needle but do not slip it off the needle. K the skipped st and remove the 2 sts at the same time. Rep. from *, ending P 1.

     Row 2: * K 1, P 2, K 1, P 2—rep. from *, ending K 1.

     Repeat these two rows for the desired amount of ribbing.

     Buttonholes can easily be worked into this type of ribbing when used on a cardigan.

(38)   When you wish to make an article in an untried or complicated pattern stitch, work out a large piece *in that pattern,* with heavier yarn and larger size needles than required for the article itself. In this way, you can become thoroughly acquainted with the appearance of the pattern stitches while working them, and there will be much better understanding of the complications when working with finer yarn.

     There is nothing more discouraging than to start a piece of knitting on a large number of stitches, and then get all mixed up in the pattern when only a half-inch or more has been worked.

DECREASING

(39)   *There are two kinds of decreases in ordinary use:* K 2 tog, which makes the resulting stitch slant to the right; and Sl 1 st, K 1 st, and pass the slipped st over the K st (SKP or Sl 1, K 1, psso), which makes the stitch slant to the left. In the case of this latter decrease, it is much simpler and the result is better if you decrease as follows: Sl the first st from the left-hand needle *knit-*wise and the second st in the same manner, onto the right-hand needle. Insert the *tip* of the left-hand needle into the *fronts* of these 2 sts which are now on the right-hand needle, and knit them together from this position.

     When making a skirt from the bottom up, the following two kinds of decreases should be alternated: K 2 tog for one round of decreases, and SKP as previously mentioned for the next round of decreases. Using just one type of decrease may result in pulling the skirt slightly on the bias, making it more difficult to block to correct shape.

     It is strongly advised to develop the good habit of using SKP at the *beginning* of a row (or shaping) and K 2 tog at the *end* of the row or shaping. This is particularly applicable to the shaping of the V on a V-neck sweater and at armhole shapings.

In lace pattern work, when decreasing at beginning and end of row, (40)
it will prove less confusing to the pattern stitch itself to decrease on
the purled side of the work.

There are times when it is necessary to take out more than one stitch (41)
at a time. In this case, it is better not to knit 3 or 4 sts tog *unless
specified in the instructions.* Instead, in taking 3 sts tog:
  Sl 1 st, K 2 tog, and pass the sl st over the K 2 tog.
In taking 4 sts tog:
  Sl 2 sts, K 2 tog, and pass the 2 sl sts over the K 2 tog.

In shaping a sleeve cap, when decreases at each side come close to- (42)
gether, be very careful not to pull these decreases too tightly. Many
sleeve caps are too tight for the armholes for which they were planned
because the decreases at the sides were too tightly worked.

INCREASING

There are many ways to increase a stitch in knitting. The one most (43)
commonly used is to knit into the front and then into the back of
the same stitch before removing it from the needle. This method of
increasing is used at edges of the work where seams are to be made,
and at places where the increase itself forms part of the scheme, such
as in raglan sleeve seams and in godets. The *yarn over* (O, or yo) is
used in raglan sleeve seams when an openwork seam is desired. However, there are many instances where you do not wish the increase to
show, such as in a skirt or in the body of a blouse or jacket. Just as in
decreasing, an increase may be made to slant either to the left or
to the right.

To Make an Increase to the Right (Fig. 10), proceed as follows:
Before working the number of sts designated, turn your work on the
left-hand needle slightly toward you so that you can see the back of
the work over the top of the needle itself. Insert the right-hand needle-
point into the *back* of the stitch *below* the stitch on the left-hand
needle and knit this little bump as a stitch, *from the top down.* Then
knit the stitch on the needle above it.

To Make an Increase to the Left (Fig. 11), proceed as follows:
Work every st to the point where the increase is to be made. Then
insert the left-hand needle-point, *from back to front* of work, under
the stitch *below* the stitch just made on the right-hand needle. Simply
push back on this one thread, and you will find that this will make an
extra stitch on the left-hand needle. Knit into the *back* of this stitch.

These methods of increasing are especially important and useful

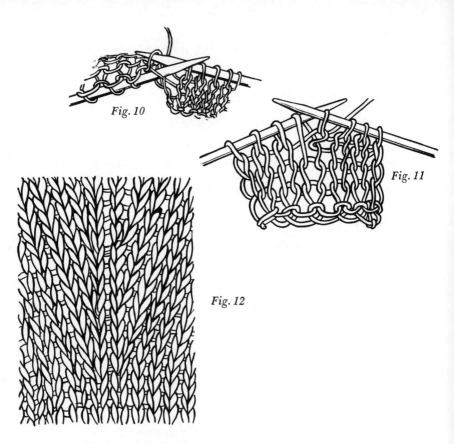

Fig. 10

Fig. 11

Fig. 12

when working a blouse or skirt in plain Stockinette Stitch where increases are certain to show when done in the first manner mentioned (i.e., by knitting into the front and back of the same st, which makes a little unsightly purled-looking bump at point of increase).

In a skirt made from the waist down and requiring the use of increases, these increases *must* be made as invisible as possible. Depending upon the style of the skirt (panels divided by a purled st or set of purled or pattern sts, or by a marked in plain Stockinette Stitch), you should increase to the *left* when *approaching* the marker or purled sts, and to the *right* when *going away* from point of increase (Fig. 12).

The methods of increasing just mentioned should *not* be used when an increase is made every second row or round, such as in the raglan seamline of a sweater. The seamline is apt to pucker.

MARKERS

Horizontal Markers. A very simple way to keep track of increase and (44) decrease rows is to work a few sts at the beginning of the row, then (Fig. 13), using a small length of thread or wool yarn of light weight and sharply contrasting color, work this thread in conjunction with the regular yarn for 3 or 4 sts. Leave this thread in the work until it is finished. It can easily be removed when work has been completed. This method of marking is especially useful for afghans, where strips must be exactly the same length as to number of rows. In such cases, a marker every ten rows will facilitate counting. (The same applies to crocheting.)

Vertical Markers. When you wish to make a division in number of sts (45) while working a knitted article, a marker should be used. Ring markers are most useful in these circumstances. If these are not avail-

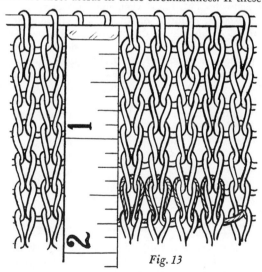

Fig. 13

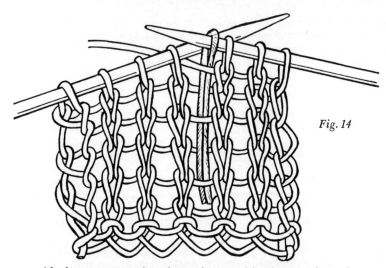

Fig. 14

able, however, use a long loop of yarn, with a knot at the *end,* not up tight against the needle. This loop, when used properly, can save a great amount of needless counting of stitches. Place a loop (or ring marker) at the point specified in the directions. On each row (Fig. 14), slip the loop (or ring marker) from the left-hand needle to the right-hand needle, drawing yarn in *back* of the marker-thread, thus weaving it through the work as you go along. When using a circular needle, draw yarn in back of marker thread on the first round and in front of it on the second round. Alternate these two rounds to keep the marker thread running through the work. When work is as long as the marker thread itself, clip off the knot at the end, and the loop will continue to slip through the work as before.

(46)   When working a pattern stitch in conjunction with Stockinette Stitch, place a marker between the Stockinette portion and the pattern portion (or portions). This marker division will eliminate the difficulty of determining where the pattern stitch begins and ends.

SLIPPING STITCHES

(47)   *When decreasing, slip the stitch knitwise.* This type of decrease holds true in lacemaking, in turning heels, and in decreasing at gussets and toes of socks; also at beginnings of rows where decreases occur. How-

ever, *when a pattern stitch* involves the slipping of a stitch *to obtain a fabric appearance, stitches must be slipped purlwise* so that, on the next row, the stitches which were slipped will be on the needle in the correct position for working.

There are only three instances when all stitches are not to be worked (48) (except, of course, in a pattern where slipped stitches are required for a desired effect). In other words, *do not slip the first stitch of a row,* as so many knitters have been taught to do, except:

   a) When an edge, such as the border of a cardigan, is worked in Garter, Seed, or any comparable stitch, in contrast to Stockinette Stitch in the body. Many knitters find it difficult to keep the edge firm. In this instance, the first st *may* be slipped instead of worked, *and slipped knit wise,* thus keeping the edge of the work straight and smooth.

   b) When decreasing to the left (see Tip 39).

   c) When turning on short rows.

JOINING YARN

When joining smooth yarns, try at all times to avoid tying yarn (49) together at any point except at the edges of the work, where the ends of yarn can be run into the seam when finishing. However, crinkly or nubby yarns may be joined with no ill effect, by tying a square knot right up against the needle at any point in the work.

   In skirts and socks, joining of wool in the work cannot be avoided, so proceed as follows. Overlap the two ends of yarn about six inches. Knit (or work in pattern) for about 6 or 8 sts with the double yarn, and work these double threads off together on the next round. Make these joins at the side of a skirt (or at the sole or back of sock) whenever possible.

Leave at least three inches whenever tying in a new piece of yarn. (50) Tie a square knot up against the needle. These three inches can easily be threaded into a yarn needle and worked into the seam edge. This suggestion applies most particularly to the making of argyle patterns.

HOW TO MEASURE WORK

To Measure Work in Progress. Lay your work down on a flat surface (51) with the needle at your left. Using a non-shrink, non-stretch tape measure, place the end of the tape just *under* the needle and measure *down* to the starting point, or to the point indicated in the instructions (Fig. 13). Do *not* stretch your knitting. Simply *smooth* your work out as it naturally would lie. Don't cheat yourself by trying to make your work measure more than it really does. You might only have to rip it and do it over again. *Never hold work up to measure it.* When an article such as a skirt or coat may stretch from weight of material, discontinue working at about two to three inches of required length. Let work hang for a few days to allow the knitting to stretch in length naturally. Then, again, measure work on a flat surface to ascertain correct measurement.

(52)   *To Measure an Armhole Correctly.* Nearly all directions specify measuring the armhole *straight up from the first bound-off stitches.* Follow Tip 44, working in a marker on the same row where you bind off for the armhole, about two inches in from the last bound-off stitch. When time to measure the armhole, measure *down from the needle* to this marker.

SIMPLEST STITCHES IN GENERAL USE

(53)   *Garter Stitch.* Knit all sts in every row. (In circular knitting, you must knit one round and purl one round.)

Stockinette Stitch. Knit all sts in one row, and purl all sts in the return row. Alternate these two rows throughout. (In circular knitting, knit all sts in every round.)

Seed, Moss, or Rice Stitch. They are all one and the same. For the first row, K 1, P 1 alternately across the row. On each succeeding row, each stitch with purled side toward you is knitted and each stitch with knit side toward you is purled.

(54)   *When working cables, unless otherwise specifically directed* in the instructions, start *row count* as follows: purled, or wrong side of work– *row one.* This will assure that every odd-numbered row will come on the wrong side of the work and every even-numbered row on the right side of the work. This method of counting rows should make the work less confusing when making the cable row itself, as it will automatically throw the cable onto the even-numbered row and on the right side of the work.

(55)   When making a cable, slip the desired number of sts onto the cable-stitch holder, keeping the curve in the holder down. When the sts are on (Fig. 15), turn the needle-points of the holder down and very lightly stick the left-hand point of the holder into the knitting to

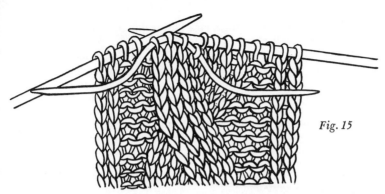

Fig. 15

keep it firmly in position. Work the next number of sts called for and then, instead of knitting the sts from the holder (which so many knitters find quite awkward), slip the sts from the holder back onto the left-hand needle and then knit them off from this. To keep the holder readily available when working a number of cables in the row, stick the holder lightly into the work, taking care that it does not split the threads of the knitting.

Simulated Knitting in Crochet. This stitch is particularly useful in (56) making belts and straps, where the appearance of knitting is desired but extra thickness and firmness are called for. Following directions for *afghan stitch* in crocheting, insert the hook through the stitch from front to back of work instead of picking up the vertical loop as in regular afghan stitch.

BINDING OFF

In binding off in a series (shoulder shaping, tops of sleeves, etc.), (57) bind off your first number of sts on each side as usual. In every succeeding bind-off, *slip* the first st, do not work it. This will give less of a step-up, more of a straight line.

To avoid that almost inevitable little point at the two sides of the top of a sleeve cap, instead of binding off all sts on the very last row, bind off only half of them on one row, and the remaining half on the return row, thus making the top of the cap more rounded and the ending thread at very center of cap. This will help in the fitting of the sleeve into the armhole.

Always bind off in pattern, i.e., follow the pattern stitches, knit or (58) purl, yarn over or slip stitch, etc. This is especially important when binding off ribbing around a neckline.

(59) When binding off a large number of sts (such as at the bottom of a skirt) you may find that binding off with a crochet hook is much quicker and easier. Proceed as follows. Holding yarn in left hand as in crocheting, insert hook into the first stitch on the left-hand needle and pull yarn through this stitch, slipping it from the needle. From this point on, work as follows. Insert the hook into next stitch, hook the yarn through the stitch on the needle and also through the stitch on the hook, slipping the stitch from the needle as you work. Of course, you must be careful to keep the edge thus bound off as loose as the knitted work itself.

NECKLINE DIVISION (Back and Front)

(60) To make both halves of one piece at the same time, divide work in the center by knitting in pattern to the exact center of piece, binding off the center st if there is an uneven number of sts in the total number before division. Tie in another ball of yarn at this point and work to the end of the row. This second ball of yarn is used to work one half of the garment and the first ball is used to work the first half. Thus, increases and decreases, bind-offs or other shapings at both sides are made simultaneously, eliminating confusion. Never put your work down without finishing *both* sections. You might forget which side to work next if you stopped at the neck edge!

(61) Ordinarily the V neckline on a man's sweater is started about one inch from the first bind-off at the armhole. However, in some cases the V is started much lower in the body, or slightly higher if a closer neckline is desired. In each case, use your row gauge to determine how close together your decreases must be made at the neckline. The shorter the neckline, the closer together must be your decreases.

PICKING UP STITCHES

(62) This term is misleading in the extreme, but is so generally used in all knitting directions that it has become the rule. It is actually a knitting operation, using the *needle and yarn* to make stitches in an edge of work that has already been completed. There are two accepted methods of picking up stitches:

    1. Tie in yarn at the point given in the instructions and hold the knitted work in the left hand. Using the yarn and one needle,

insert the needle-point into the work, *at least two threads in* from the edge so that there will be no holes in the finished work. Wrap yarn around needle and pull loop through just as if you were knitting stitches from a needle (Fig. 16).

2. Using a crochet hook, insert the hook into the knitted article, *at least two threads in* from the edge, pull loop through, and slip this loop onto the knitting needle. Some knitters, using this method, find it easier to pick up several sts at one time onto the hook, *then* slip them off from the back of the crochet hook onto the knitting needle.

The two main points to remember are these: Pick up the necessary number of sts according to the instructions or, if no number is given, pick up according to gauge (see Tip 22), and *do not get too close to the edge.*

To determine the number of sts to be picked up, measure the edge (63) of the work where the sts are to be taken, multiply the number of inches by the gauge used in the body of sweater, and use the result obtained for the number of sts. That is, if one edge of the V on a V-neck sweater measures 10 inches and you have worked the body of the sweater on an 8-st gauge, you would pick up about 80 sts along that edge.

When sts have been put on holders at a neckline, there is apt to be (64) a resulting looseness of sts when approaching the ribbed finish. To avoid this, pick up an extra st at each end of the needle onto which these sts have been transferred. On the first row of ribbing, knit or purl this extra st together with the end stitch that was originally on the needle.

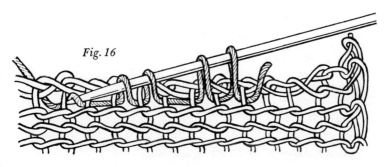

Fig. 16

NECKLINE SHAPING

(65)   *Finishing the Round Neck of a Pullover.* Instead of binding off sts at back and front of neck, leave these sts on a stitch-holder so that maximum stretch may be obtained when picking up for round neck of a pullover with no opening at the back or front.

     If you wish to have a pullover with no opening and a *high* round neck, it may be wise to shape the *back* of the neck as well as the front. Do this shaping just before the shoulder shaping at *back* of neck and about one and a half to two inches before the shoulder shaping at *front* of neck. It is most advisable to follow this procedure on a baby's or child's sweater, as it gives more room to pick up extra sts around the neckline, thus saving much howling from baby when the sweater is pulled over ears and such.

(66)   *Finishing the Neckline of a V-Neck Sweater.* Tie in yarn at the left shoulder seamline. Using 10-inch DP needles (or a circular needle of correct length), knit up your sts (Tip 62) according to gauge (Tip 22), inserting needle at least two threads in from the edge of the work. In other words, pretend that the sts on the neck edge are sts on a needle and knit *into* the knitted edge. When you feel that there is too large a space, which might make a hole in the finished work, go into a st in back of that space, a st which will make a tighter hole.

     REMEMBER, GETTING TOO CLOSE TO THE EDGE WHEN PICKING UP STITCHES IS A DEFINITE FAULT.

     When all sts have been picked up on one edge of the V, count the number of sts on this needle (or to this point, if you are using a circular needle, where a marker should be placed to show point of V). Using another needle, and picking up from the V to the right

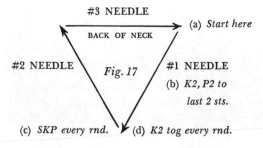

shoulder seam, pick up two more or two less sts (if K 2, P 2 ribbing is to be used) than were picked up on the other edge. Pick up one more or one less if K 1, P 1 ribbing is to be used. Knit, st for st, across the back of the neck, on a third needle. Number your needles as follows:

No. 1, going down to the V from the left shoulder seam.

No. 2, going up from the V to the right shoulder seam.

No. 3, going across the back of the neck (Fig. 17). You will be working round and round from this point, just as on a sock. On No. 1 needle, K 2, P 2 to the last 2 sts. Always, *every* round, K the last 2 sts tog at this point. At the beginning of the No. 2 needle, *every* round, SKP (see Tip 40), pulling the slipped st very firmly to prevent a hole from developing in the mitering at this point. Proceed in pattern of K 2, P 2 but starting, after this decrease, with whichever st or sts you

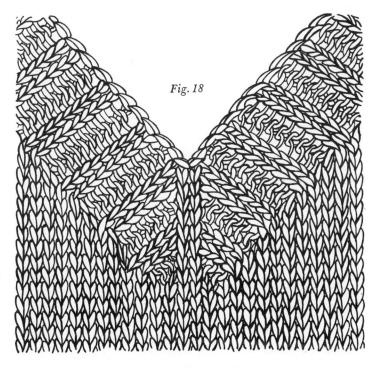

Fig. 18

ended with on No. 1 needle before the decrease of K 2 tog. This will make the sts either side of the miter symmetrical, perfectly matched, and the sts at *end* of the No. 2 needle end with P 2. In every succeeding round there will be one less st of the original ribbing on each side of the V line (Fig. 18). When binding off, continue to make these two decreases at the same points. In making a K 1, P 1 ribbing, substitute K 1, P 1 for the K 2, P 2 above.

ASSEMBLING

(67) *How to Join Pieces of a Knitted Sweater.* To join the seams of a sweater, you should use the same yarn as used in the sweater, unless the yarn is exceptionally bulky. In this case, use a lighter-weight yarn of matching color.

To join side seams, hold the two right sides of work together, the wrong sides out, and slip-stitch with a crochet hook; i.e., put hook through a st in one side of sweater seam, one st in from the edge, and then through the corresponding st in the other side of sweater; in other words, work into corresponding rows of knitting on either side. Catching yarn with hook, draw through both sides of sweater *and straight through the loop on hook.* Do the same thing in the next row of knitting, and repeat this procedure along the entire seam. This method of crocheting a sweater together produces *slightly more give* than a seam which is sewed, and *holds a little firmer without ripping,* especially when the garment is to be worn by an active person.

Join sleeve seams in the same manner. Weave or graft shoulder seams together (Tip 68). Set in sleeves as follows: With the *sleeve side* facing you, pin center top of sleeve to shoulder seam. Pin underarm seam to underarm seam of sweater. Then, with *sleeve side* still facing you, pin *from* the underarm seam *toward* the shoulder seam, easing in any fullness two inches each side of top of sleeve. With *body side* of sweater facing you, work seam in slip stitch as at side seams. This insures a smooth straight seam, as you can follow the rows of knitting as a guide. *It is earnestly advised* to set sts close together rather than to space them widely. A sleeve, if set in with large spaces between sts, is apt to draw too tightly. This makes the armhole smaller than planned and liable to draw uncomfortably when worn.

Next, take a tapestry needle and, on the wrong side of the article, weave into the back of the work all the threads which have been left loose.

NEVER JOIN ANY SEAM BY OVERCASTING OR SINGLE CROCHET. If you prefer to *sew* a seam rather than to crochet it, use a running back stitch, being careful not to draw the stitches too tight. Any type of joining should have as much give as the knitting itself.

GRAFTING

When joining two edges together, particularly two bound-off edges   (68) which have been worked in Stockinette Stitch, grafting gives a much neater-looking seam than sewing or crocheting them together.

Thread a tapestry needle with matching yarn. Hold the two edges together with both right sides facing you. Observe both pieces carefully and you will see that, on the side farthest away from you there are chains going *away* from you, and on the side nearest you there are chains coming *toward* you. Each chain is a stitch (Fig. 19). Fasten your thread at edge of work and insert needle under the first chain coming toward you on the near side, *just inside the bound-off edge.* Insert the needle *horizontally.* Draw the needle through and then insert it under the matching chain going away from you on the far side. Draw the needle through. On succeeding stitches, the needle is inserted into the same point where the thread came out the stitch before. This grafting is *always* done from right to left, and the needle is *always* inserted under the stitches *horizontally* (Fig. 20).

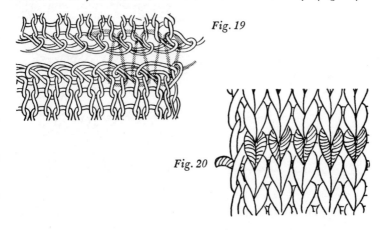

Fig. 19

Fig. 20

When grafting the front and back of a shoulder together, it is advisable to start at the armhole or sleeve edge.

FINISHING

(69)   *Working a Crocheted Border.* Many times a crocheted band is preferred on the front closing of a cardigan or some similar article. It has a decided advantage over a knitted border in that it is thicker and stronger and needs no ribbon facing.

When working crochet on knitting, the gauge is again very important. It is wise to practice on a knitted swatch of the same yarn, worked on the same needles, before proceeding to work on the garment itself. Choosing the correct size crochet hook is important. The border must lie flat and smooth, not ruffling or puckering (Fig. 21).

Always work the initial row of crochet *with the right side* of the knitted work facing you. As in picking up stitches (Tip 65), the crochet hook must be inserted into the knitting *at least two threads in* from the edge. There should be three single crochet stitches to each four rows of knitting if the correct gauge is followed. Therefore, start the first stitch in the first row of knitting, the second stitch in the second row of knitting, the third stitch in the third row of knitting and make no stitch in the fourth row (i.e., skip each fourth row of knitting in your first crocheted row). Each succeeding row, ch 1 to turn, and then work into every crochet stitch with single crochet. It is wise to have the finished crocheted border *very slightly*

Fig. 21

tighter than the knitted work. This can easily be pressed and stretched to correct proportion.

There are times when ribbing, as a finish, is not desired on a V neck-line. When you wish to have a dressier look on a blouse, proceed as follows: (70)

Pick up the required number of sts in the usual manner, leaving a marker at center of the V. On each purl row, P 2 tog at each side of the marker, and on each knit row, K 2 tog at each side of marker. Work in Stockinette Stitch in this manner for the desired width. Purl one row on the right side or knit one row on the wrong side for a hemline. Then increase one st each side of marker *every row* for the same number of rows, plus one. Bind off and turn back to form a hem. Hem the bound-off edge to the seamline which was made by picking up sts.

Inserting Zippers in Knitted or Crocheted Articles. Make one row   (71)
of single crochet around or down the edges of the opening where the zipper is to be inserted. Pin the closed zipper into place according to the directions which come with the zipper package, but *do not stretch* the edges of the knitted work; instead, *pull* them slightly for the best results. Sew into place with mercerized cotton thread. The crocheted edges should cover the zipper. Therefore, if necessary, work an extra row of single crochet on one edge after the insertion of the zipper.

BLOCKING SIMPLE SWEATERS AND BLOUSES

Lay a damp towel on a flat surface. Shape the garment to be blocked   (72)
on the towel, making liberal use of the tape measure and the measurements in your directions, to insure proper fit. If the blouse or sweater is to be close-fitting, the shape of the garment itself, on the towel, should be followed just as it is. However, if you wish to have a more loosely fitting garment, especially around the bustline, be sure to see that the full bustline measurement continues to at least four to five inches below the actual bustline.

Use rust-proof tacks and tissue paper (Tip 76) to hold garment in shape. Cover with a damp towel or heavy cloth and leave until all pieces are dry. No extra weight or pressure is necessary, as the moisture and weight of the damp cloth will make the article smooth.

When blocking a sweater with ribbing at waist and/or sleeves, try   (73)
to avoid covering the ribbing with the damp towels. The moisture

41

and pressure are apt to spread the ribbing, which is not desirable.

(74) When article to be blocked is not too large, the use of a window screen is a time and space saver. Use a good grade of copper or aluminum wire screening and paint with hard-finish enamel paint. Rest on backs of two chairs or some similar place where air can circulate freely under the screen. Cover with a heavy cloth or towel, and then block garment as directed.

For faster drying, place an oscillating fan on a stand close to the side of the screen so that the air can circulate under and over the screen. *Never, under any circumstances, even with white yarn, put a garment in the sun to dry.* It is a well-established fact that wool yarns, in particular, will sunburn.

TAILORED FINISHING AND BLOCKING

(75) *Note.* This method is recommended in assembling, blocking, and finishing fitted garments such as dressy blouses, dresses (either one- or two-piece), and suits, *made of wool or similar yarns.* It is a skilled operation, and a basic knowledge of dressmaking and tailoring is extremely desirable. Each piece of the garment is blocked separately and then assembled by basting the pieces together with *wool yarn.* Always sew the pieces on final joining with yarn of same color and texture, unless large nubby yarns are used. In this case, threading even a large needle with this type of yarn is almost impossible, and sewing with it simply cannot be done easily. It is suggested that light-weight (crewel-weight) tapestry yarn be used if possible. This is available in a great range of colors and shades.

Procedure. Cut separate pieces of heavy unglazed wrapping paper to exact same size and shape as each separate piece of the garment, excluding the skirt only when it is made on a circular needle. Baste each knitted piece, right side down, onto its paper counterpart with yarn, having the long stitches of the basting on the paper side. (This leaves no basting marks on the work.) Lay piece, paper side down, on a large ironing surface, well padded. Place a damp pressing cloth on the knitted work and steam the piece thoroughly *without allowing the weight of the iron to rest on the cloth too heavily.* Remove pieces from paper and baste the back to the front (or fronts) of blouse, again with yarn, and try on, *wrong side out.* Any necessary adjustments (tucks, shirrings, darts, etc.) should be made at this point in the fitting operation. Sew the seams and/or darts with yarn in a running back stitch, or follow Tip 67 and crochet in slip-stitch, following the fitting lines and making sure that the stitches do not bind. Any material left in the seam should be pressed back on the final pressing.

Next, baste sleeve seams and baste sleeve into armhole, leaving about four inches open at top of sleeve, two inches each side of shoulder seams of body, to allow for any adjustments needed. Try on again and pin this portion in, easing it into the remaining part of the armhole. Remove, baste, then join seams as on body. When all seams have been joined and all body fittings made, you are ready to put on the finishing touches.

Unless hems are indicated at the finishing (or open) edges, work one or two rows of single crochet around these edges to keep them from rolling up (see Tip 69).

Follow Tip 71 if zippers are to be inserted.

At back of neck or on shoulder seams, narrow tape may be needed to retain the shape and keep the original fit of the garment. Using mercerized cotton sewing thread, whip these tapes into position. *Note carefully that thread is used only at points where material other than the knitted work itself is involved.*

When *ribbon or banding* is used at the waistline, don't put it on by guesswork. Again, try the garment on, wrong side out, and pin this ribbon in. Make necessary adjustments, *then* take it off and whip ribbon in.

If buttonholes have been worked into the knitting, it is advisable to face both the button and buttonhole side with ribbon. This ribbon should be put in as one of the last bits of finishing. Just as in applying ribbon at the waistline, the ribbon must be fitted to the edges before cutting and applying, to make sure that the front edges do not "droop." The two pieces of ribbon should, naturally, be of the exact same length and pinned, basted, and whipped in. (Leave basting threads in the buttonhole side until final pressing.) Then comes the *making of the buttonholes.* Pin the buttonhole side to the button side very carefully. Mark the position of the buttonholes in the ribbon of the buttonhole side. Remove the ribbon and work the buttonholes to desired size with machine or by hand. Cut holes and then apply again to position, baste carefully to match the holes in the knitting and the ribbon, and whip the edges. Overcast the holes made in the ribbon to the knitted buttonholes, making stitches as unnoticeable as possible.

Skirt Made in Separate Panels. Block and put together, using same method as in finishing the jacket or blouse. The skirt may have an opening at side, with or without zipper, just as a skirt made on a circular needle. If belting is used, it is applied exactly as you would apply it on a skirt made of woven material.

If there is no opening at the side and you wish the skirt to be supported with elastic in a casing, proceed as follows: Work about one inch of single crochet around the top, then turn work around to the wrong side without breaking thread. Make a chain of three-quarters of an inch and carry this chain diagonally to the base of the band made by the crochet and slip-stitch into the work. Make another chain of the same length and carry this chain again to the top edge and fasten. Repeat this process around the top of the band. Run a piece of elastic (from three-quarters of an inch to an inch wide), through the beading and sew the ends together.

Skirt Made on Circular Needle. Finish top of skirt as described, *before* blocking. Do the blocking on a large enough space to accommodate the entire skirt—on a rug or a large table which has been thoroughly protected from heat and dampness. A folding asbestos table-protector, covered with heavy paper and cloth, is ideal.

Cut a piece of heavy cotton tape to half your waistline measurement, another one to half your hipline measurement, and a third to measure half the width you wish to have at the bottom of the skirt. For example, if your waistline is 28 inches, your hipline 38 inches and the bottom of the skirt is to be 66 inches wide, you would cut one tape 14 inches, one 19 inches, and the third 33 inches.

Cut five pieces of tape to the desired length of your skirt and follow these seven steps (Fig. 22) :

1. Press the waistline tape along the top of skirt, using tacks as in Tip 76, stretching or easing in the top edge.

2. Using one of the skirt-length tapes, press one tack into center top of skirt through the tape and pull taut down center line. Fasten this tape into center of bottom edge of skirt, and fasten down.

3. At this point, establish the center of the tape to be used at the bottom width and press the bottom tack (the last one inserted) into this tape at the same point. Stretch this tape out to the sides to establish the bottom width of skirt, and fasten down temporarily at each end.

4. Using the hipline tape, measure down from the waistline *to three inches above the fullest part of hipline* and draw this tape

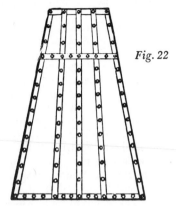

Fig. 22

across the work itself at this point, just *over* the work. This tape is to be used later on.

5. Take plenty of tissue paper, crush and roll, and insert into the two folded sides. Press one of the length tapes into top of skirt, just inside of paper at side, and another into the other side. Stretch these tapes down, diagonally, one to each end of the width tape at bottom.

6. Fasten the last two tapes to the top of skirt, between the center and outside tapes. Pull straight and fasten to the bottom tape.

7. Shape the skirt to these eight tapes, press tacks into all tapes about two inches apart, shaping the knitted material to fit the form thus made. Cover all with damp turkish towels and leave until thoroughly dry.

Using a warm, *not hot*, iron, press all necessary points—seams (pressing back seam allowances), shoulders, tops of sleeves, etc.— using a sleeve board or a tailor's mitten.

The use of a steam iron at these points is most desirable. If used, set at *medium* heat.

WASHING AND BLOCKING

In blocking simple blouses and sweaters, press all pieces on wrong   (76)
side very lightly with a steam iron or with a dry iron over a damp cloth, making sure not to stretch any part of the garment unless specified by your tape measure and carefully "rolling" out the side

45

and top seam edges. *Do not press* ANY *ribbing* unless this ribbing is used specifically as trim.

If article is soiled, have it cleaned or wash carefully in tepid water with any good *mild* soap powder, liquid or· detergent. There are many products on the market that are made for the sole purpose of washing fine woolens; better to use one of these special kinds. Rinse all articles *thoroughly* in water of the same temperature. *Do not leave any soap or detergent in the article,* despite suggestions on the package or bottle to do so. It may leave the knitted piece a little fluffier temporarily, but may eventually injure the wool irreparably. Also, *never rub* the garment while washing. Squeeze the suds through and through until all soil has been removed. If the article is *very* soiled, it is far preferable to wash it in two or three different sudsings rather than to use a large amount of cleansing product just once. More soil can be more safely and surely removed in this manner.

NEVER hold garment up while wet, as weight of water will stretch it. Press out as much water as possible, and then lay garment in a large turkish towel, folding towel around it. Wring the towel *hard.* This will not harm the garment, as you are wringing the towel, not the garment. Put the garment on a dry towel on a flat surface; pat out to shape, using tape measure to insure proper fit. *NEVER stick pins into the edges of knitting.* If you *must* fasten it down, use absolutely *rustproof* long-pointed thumbtacks, pressed through a strip of cotton tape or heavy cloth. To avoid that "creased-in" look at seams and in sleeves, use lots of tissue paper, rolled and slightly crushed, and put it down the side seams, in the sleeves, and at shoulder seams. Press tacks *inside* of paper at sides. *Remember this* about washing woolens: *it is the moisture left in the wool after washing that causes most shrinkage.*

(77)   A good way to wring all moisture out of wool or a knitted piece is to wrap it in a large towel and put through a wringer which has been slightly loosened.

(78)   When washing articles that have been made in Garter Stitch, remember that *they will stretch quite a bit* because of the nature of the stitch. You will have to *push* them into shape, rather than pat out to shape.

(79)   *When washing and blocking a cardigan,* baste front closing together on both edges *with yarn, never with thread.* Thread is apt to cut wool yarn. Wash and block as directed. When dry, the front edges will be the same length and not stretched out of shape.

While moisture does cause most of the shrinkage in a garment, it (80)
is also true that stretching a garment too much or too often while
it is damp will also cause eventual shrinkage.

When blocking a baby cap, wrap a pincushion, or a bowl about the (81)
size of a baby's head, with a small turkish towel. Baste any turned-
back parts with wool yarn, and wash the cap. Shape it around the form.

Before washing any article, run a length of yarn, doubled, into the (82)
side seam or sleeve seam. Later on, if repairs are needed, you can
remove and use this yarn, which will be of just the same shade as
the article itself.

ERRORS

When you have made the mistake of knitting a purled stitch or (83)
purling a knit stitch (or dropped a stitch), work over to that point
in the work directly above where the mistake has been made and
drop this stitch from the needle and down to the point of the mistake.
Turn the work, if necessary, to have the *knitted* side of that same
stitch facing you. Then, using a crochet hook, reach in with the hook
and pull each successive step of the ladder thus made through the
loop on the hook, one at a time. Pull the bottom loop through from
the back toward the front, being careful not to twist the loop.

When an error has been made and you must rip back by taking the (84)
knitting off the needles, it will facilitate your work if, for the pick-up
row, you use a smaller size needle than originally used. The point
of a smaller needle will slip into the stitches much more easily than
the larger needle.

When pulling out work in knitting, pull back to the row *above* the (85)
one you wish to pick up, then put your needle into the stitch below
the exposed loop, *purlwise,* holding thread in *left* hand. Pull thread
out of each stitch gently as you pick up the one underneath it. Thus
the stitches are on the needle in the correct position for working
the next row, and none are lost or dropped. However, if one stitch
should slip or drop, put your needle into *this* stitch *knitwise,* right
where it is. On the next row, the fact that the stitch is twisted on the
needle will indicate that something is wrong at this point, and you
can correct the error here.

If you find that you have cast on too tightly on socks or any similar (86)
article which requires more than the usual stretch at the edge, you
can cut off the whole cast-on row or snip one stitch and pull a thread

about two rows back from the edge. Tie in yarn and, using a crochet hook, make one row of very loose slip-stitch in crochet, catching every loop of the knitted edge.

(87)   *If a Stockinette Stitch sweater is too short from armhole to ribbing at waist,* open the side seams of sweater and pull a thread through across the entire piece of work (back and front) two rows above the ribbed border, cutting off the ribbing from the main part of the blouse. To do this, snip one little stitch near the edge of the work at seam and pull the yarn gently, but firmly, just as you would pull a thread in a piece of material. Pick up sts at the bottom edge of Stockinette on one needle and the sts at top of ribbing on another needle, holding the ribbing portion in reserve. Attach yarn to the top piece and work as much Stockinette Stitch as desired for altered length. Join this portion to tne ribbing with Kitcnener Stitch (see Plain Socks, page 56).

Any pattern-stitch sweater may be *shortened* by this procedure. *No* pattern-stitch sweater may be successfully *lengthened,* as all sts will be half a st off pattern.

(88)   *Straightening a Vertical Edge.* If it should happen that the edge of work, such as the front edge of a cardigan, is loose and not neat-looking, this looseness may be remedied by working one or two rows of slip-stitch in crochet at the very edge, on the wrong side of the work.

SPECIAL TOUCHES

(89)   *Buttonholes* (see **Fig.** 23). If you have trouble *making a neat-looking buttonhole* with no unsightly loop at either side, bind off the required

Fig. 23

number of sts and, on the return row where the directions say to cast on the same number of sts as were bound off, proceed as follows: Turn work completely around to the other side. Follow Tip 31 for the number of sts to be cast on. Then, pick up a loop *from under the first st which was bound off* and slip this st onto the left-hand needle. Turn work around again and finish the row. On the next row, knit the extra loop which was pulled up from the bound-off row, together with the following st (the last one which was cast on), inserting needle into the *fronts* of these 2 sts. When coming to the first st which was cast on, as in Tip 31, knit into the back of the loose st to pull it tight.

When buttons are used on the front of a jacket or blouse and they (90) are set far apart, it is wise to sew a snap fastener between each button, or make an invisible eye with thread of same color and use a hook on the underside of the buttonhole edge. This helps to avoid any gap between buttons. In case you do not wish to make button-holes, but want to have the appearance of a buttoned garment, simply sew snap fasteners under the buttons and at corresponding points on the other side. This eliminates the chance that buttonholes knitted into the piece might be rather awkwardly placed when the jacket is blocked and finished. In this way, the buttons can be placed at exactly the right distances for the best over-all effect.

Making Slits during Progress of Work. When you wish to make a (91) pocket slit, a large buttonhole, or a thumb of a mitten or glove, and you wish to continue to work this division later, drop the main-color yarn at this point and, with another piece of yarn *of a sharply contrasting color,* work the required number of sts. Slip these sts back onto the left-hand needle, pick up the main-color yarn, and knit these colored sts. This colored yarn will be pulled out later, and the resulting loops picked up from both the bottom and the top edge on two different needles, these sts to be worked in any type of finish desired.

Bias Binding. When a tailored finish is desired and a crocheted edge (92) does not seem suitable, try this as a trim edging. Make a bias binding as follows and apply to the edge: Cast on 2 sts. Working in Stockinette Stitch, increase 1 st at the beginning of every knit row until your total number of sts measures 1½ inches or desired width (see Tip 22). Then increase 1 st at beginning and decrease 1 st at end of every knit row. Purl all sts on return row. Repeat for desired length, bearing in mind that this piece is going to stretch considerably more than a straight edge. Decrease 1 st at end of every knit row until 2 sts remain. Bind off. Steam-press thoroughly, and then apply to the edge of work just as you would apply any bias binding to clothing made of other material.

(93) *Knitted Hem.* Many instructions call for a knitted hem during progress of work. In some cases, this hem is apt to be too full and "push out" when the final hemming has been completed. Unless the instructions have already specified the following procedure, it is wiser to use a smaller size needle for the working of the hem portion, including the "turning" row. Then change to the regular size needle called for in the instructions for the main body of work.

(94) You may find a blouse or dress pattern you would like to make, but may prefer a *closer-fitting sleeve* than the one provided for in the instructions. In this case, you should make fewer increases and, therefore, there would be fewer sts on the needles than called for in the instructions when you reach the top of the sleeve. It is possible, then, that you might have too few sts *and rows* at the sleeve cap to decrease according to the directions. To make certain of having a long enough sleeve cap to fit the armhole, proceed as follows. On each side of the sleeve, bind off the number of sts mentioned in the directions. From this point on, decrease 1 st each end of needle every *fourth* or *sixth* row, using row gauge (Tip 23), until the sleeve cap measures 1½ inches less than measurement at the armhole of the blouse. In other words, if the armhole measurement is 8 inches, work the sleeve cap in this manner until it measures 6½ inches. Then, bind off 2 or 3 sts each side of the top of the cap, two or three times, and then bind off all sts.

(95) When knitting a shaped blouse and you wish to have the *waistline fit snugly,* change to a smaller size needle when you reach the waistline. Work one or two inches on this smaller needle, and change back to the regular size needle for the rest of the work.

HOW TO FOLLOW INSTRUCTIONS

(96) INSTRUCTIONS ARE NOT WRITTEN TO BE READ; THEY ARE WRITTEN TO BE FOLLOWED. Too many knitters read the whole article through, puzzling over each little aspect of the written directions, wondering why so and so happens and what the end result should be. *Do not anticipate* any step in the instructions until the one preceding it has been worked to its conclusion.

Many knitters find it very difficult to read instructions in knitting   (97)
books. It should be realized that in these books instructions must
take up a minimum amount of space because of the cost of produc-
tion, and, therefore, all directions for one piece of the garment are
consolidated into one small paragraph. It is a simple matter to break
this paragraph down into small parts by writing each sentence separately on a large sheet of paper, using a typewriter if possible, and
leaving a space on the paper between each sentence. Each small
operation is then seen in its entirety, is more easily understood, and
is therefore much less confusing to read and to apply. Keeping this
thought in mind, apply the same method to breaking down a pattern
stitch into each separate operation, keeping each row separated from
the one preceding it.

MAKING LIFE HAPPIER FOR YOUR INSTRUCTOR

If you know which pattern, in which book, you wish to follow, and   (98)
you have bought the yarn you are going to use, you will save time
for yourself and your instructor if you have your swatch made before
you approach her table. Work at least 24 sts in the type of stitch
you wish to make, with the yarn you are going to use, for at least
2 inches. Do not bind off; leave sts on the needle. She can take your
gauge as soon as your turn comes, and you can be off about your
business much sooner because of this small bit of preparation on
your part.

Try, at all times, to keep a light-colored ball of worsted or some   (99)
similar yarn in your knitting bag, this to be used in trying out the
different stitches or methods that your instructor may indicate. It is
much easier to observe your work as it progresses if you work with
heavy yarn and large needles. It is also much easier and saves time
for the instructor to pick up a pair of needles with a considerable
piece of work on them when she wishes to demonstrate a point of
procedure.

If you really wish to be fully prepared, have about 32 sts already
worked (for about 2 inches) in Stockinette Stitch. This number of
sts should certainly be sufficient for any kind of demonstration or
teaching procedure.

Please don't go to your instructor and say that you wish to make a   (100)
blouse or sweater for a friend or relative size 14, 10, 16, or any size

you may consider to be the right one. The size dress or shirt the person may wear gives no real indication to the instructor as to the *knitted* size required. *If the garment is to fit properly, proper measurements must be given* (see Tip 20). If for some reason they cannot be taken, try to bring with you some well-fitting blouse or sweater belonging to the person for whom the knitted garment is to be made. Measurements can be fairly accurately judged in this case. However, height of the person and the distribution of the figure must be taken into account, and instructions must be given with all these points taken into consideration. With these points in mind, you can readily see that, excellent as the instructions may be, the finished garment may not fit as perfectly as you would wish. *The best instructions require the best possible measurements.*

(101)   A little consideration on your part will produce the desired consideration on the part of the instructor. A few emphatic DON'TS are outlined here:

DON'T expect an instructor to welcome you with happy smiles when you come in for complicated instructions a half-hour before closing time. She has already been working hard for nearly the full day and can well be expected to be at a low ebb of ideas and energy.

DON'T insist on asking for *full* instructions on the first visit. Your instructor knows what tragedies of pulling out and revising are likely to be in the offing because of possible change in knitting tension on your part.

DON'T refuse to send or bring your work in for checking. It is most important that this be done, and it results in confidence and reassurance to both instructor and knitter.

DON'T get into loud discussion with your neighbor or friend. Please keep conversation as quiet as possible if there are many people at your instructor's table or in the room. All your instructions require an unharried atmosphere for the teacher, as they are the result of complicated mathematics and keen mental activity on her part.

DON'T go to your instructor during the lunchtime hours if it can possibly be avoided. It isn't fair to occupy the only hours when those who go to business can get in for instructions.

DON'T, above all, break into the instructor's or another customer's time for a small question of procedure. That "just one small question" might very conceivably require anywhere from five to twenty minutes for its solution, and the nervous tension built up might justifiably make the instructor lacking in consideration at a later date.

KNITTING WITH RIBBON

There are many kinds and textures of ribbons and about as many ways to work with them. They may be used alone or worked with yarns (see Tip 7). The methods used depend on the type of garment you wish to make.

Ribbons are manufactured from many different kinds of materials —rayon, silk, nylon, etc., and combinations of these. Some are crisp, made of taffeta or organdy; others are very soft and pliable and made of pure silk or silk-and-rayon mixture; some are woven or printed to give a tweed effect, and still others have metallic threads incorporated in the edges or center. There are "fuse-cut" ribbons and woven ribbons. All have their own particular uses, and these are defined in the instruction books, which have designs made especially to suit the texture of the ribbon and the style of the particular garment to be made. In every case, the stitch to be used is outlined and should be carefully learned and followed. As in all the preceding tips, *learn the method of making the stitch first,* get the *gauge* required in the directions, and, using the rules for measurement (Tip 20), follow all instructions very carefully.

The following are ways to work with ribbon which may be of interest to those who like to "play around" with different methods and results. If the results are desirable, and you would prefer to use one of these as against the one suggested in the pattern book, *make sure once again to obtain the correct* GAUGE specified in the instruction for the particular garment you wish to make.

1. Keeping ribbon flat, wind it around the needle, inserting the needle into the *back* of the sts on the knit rows, and purling in the regular manner on the purled rows.

2. A braided effect may be obtained by using the same method with one exception only. After inserting the needle into the st on the knit row (into *back* of st), instead of bringing ribbon toward you *under* the needle and then away, bring the ribbon toward you *over* the needle and then away from you under the needle.

3. The following method of using ribbon produces the woven effect illustrated (Fig. 24). It requires time and a great deal of patience to learn, but it can result in a really beautiful piece, worthy of the finest Paris salons. When properly executed, this stitch will produce a flat, diagonal weave with no holes appearing in the finished material; it also has less stretch than most other methods.

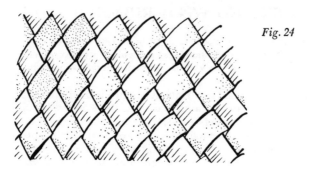

Fig. 24

Great care must be exercised in keeping the ribbon flat when winding on the needle. It is suggested that a mark be made along one surface of the ribbon for a considerable length. This will facilitate the keeping of this marked surface against the surface of the needle, thus eliminating the chance of the ribbon's being twisted while being worked.

Before starting, practice winding the ribbon around the needle, spirally, several times. You will notice that it is necessary to drop the ribbon after each turn around the needle. As in this practice winding, so you will have to drop the ribbon after each st, to readjust it for the next st, making sure that the ribbon comes out of that st flat (Fig. 25). On the purled row, the ribbon must be wound around the needle in the opposite manner from that in regular purling. As in

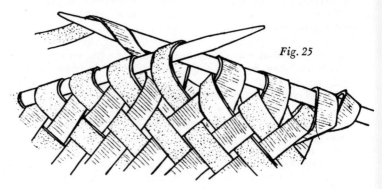

Fig. 25

knitting, keep the ribbon flat and readjust it after the completion of each st. Wind it *under* the needle *away* from you, and then *over* the needle *toward* you. Always work loosely, and *do not pull back on the ribbon.* If you are in the habit of winding yarn around any of your fingers, or holding it tightly, *you must not do so* in working with ribbon in this manner.

Always pull out several yards of ribbon ahead of your knitting. In working any ribbon stitch, the ribbon will twist from the work to the spool. Pin the ribbon to the spool and hold up to allow it to untwist. When working *this* type of stitch, the ribbon will twist one way going across the row and untwist itself on the return row. You will find that it will be less bothersome if you work to the center of your piece and then let the ribbon untwist at this point.

Clothing made with ribbon, in any type of stitch, must be just as carefully worked to gauge as that made of yarn. In working this *flat* ribbon stitch, you must make sure that the knitting is kept flat and that the correct *gauge* is obtained. The difference of half a st in an inch is of great importance, as there are so few sts to an inch in the gauge.

Following Tip 21, make a large swatch and bind off. Put this swatch right side down on a well-padded pressing board and cover it with a damp cloth. Set your iron to "silk" control and press. Remove cloth, turn to "synthetic" control, and press until thoroughly dry. Remove from pressing board and *then* check your gauge for sts and rows per inch.

To Finish Ribbon Garments. As in Tip 75, the finishing of a knitted ribbon piece requires a basic knowledge of dressmaking. Each piece must be thoroughly pressed before basting and sewing. The garment must be basted and fitted *first,* then the seams machine- or hand-stitched together, the material being treated exactly as though it were dress material. Finishing of open edges such as bottoms of skirt, blouse, sleeves, and necklines, may be worked in single crochet, just as in wool pieces. These points, and all finishing points such as seam allowances, darts, edges, etc., should be pressed as the final touch.

PLAIN SOCKS

MATERIALS

3 oz. of 3-ply sock yarn
1 set of 7-inch DP Precision Tapered Knitting Needles, No. 2
GAUGE. 7½ sts = 1 inch

To Begin. On No. 2 needles, cast on 64 sts *loosely;* 20 sts on first needle, 20 sts on second needle, and 24 sts on third needle. Join carefully, making sure not to twist sts on needles, and work round and round in K 2, P 2 ribbing for 3 inches. Then work in Stockinette Stitch (K all sts in each round) for 7 inches or until piece measures 10 inches in all.

To Make Heel. Slip the sts from one needle to the other until you have 32 sts on one needle and 16 sts on each of the other two. The 32 sts on the one needle are to be worked for the heel. Proceed as follows:

Row 1 — * K 1 st, Sl 1 st, rep from * across the row to the last 2 sts. K these 2 sts.
Row 2 — P all sts.
Repeat these two rows for 2½ inches and end on a K row; i.e., finish the K row.

To Turn Heel. P 18 sts, P 2 tog., P 1 and turn work to the right side. (There will be sts left at the end of the needle, but, *ignoring these,* use this same needle for the following row.) Then, Sl the first st, K 5, SKP and K 1. Turn work as before. Sl the first st and P to the st in front of the gap made by turning on the previous row. P these 2 sts (one on either side of the gap), together, P 1 more st and turn. Continue in this manner, always slipping the first st after turning and working to the gap, decreasing the 2 sts either side of the gap, plus knitting or purling one more st. There will be 18 sts left when all sts at the sides of the needles are used up, and you will end on a K row.

To Make Gusset. Combine all 32 sts on the two instep needles on one needle. Then, on heel you have just finished, slip the first 9 sts off onto one needle and, using the yarn at end of *last* 9 sts on original heel needle, knit up 18 sts along the side of heel (see Tip 62). Make sure the sts are evenly spaced between the heel and instep and make the last st right up close to the instep sts.

Use another needle to work across the 32 instep sts, and still another needle to pick up 18 sts along other side of heel. With this same needle, K the 9 sts from the first heel needle. Thus you have 27 sts on each of the two heel needles, and 32 sts on the instep needle.

To Decrease For Gusset. Number your needles as follows:

No. 1 needle going from the instep to the back of heel—27 sts.

No. 2 needle going from the back of heel to instep—27 sts.

No. 3 needle going across instep—32 sts.

Round 1—No. 1 needle—K 1, SKP, K to end.

No. 2 needle—K to last 3 sts, K 2 tog, K 1.

No. 3 needle—K all sts.

Round 2—K all sts on all three needles.

Repeat these two rounds until there are 16 sts on No. 1 and No. 2 needles, and 64 sts in all. Work round and round until the sock measures, from the very back of the heel, 1½ inches less than the desired length (or size) of sock.

To Toe Off:

Round 1—No. 1 needle—K 1, SKP, K to end.

No. 2 needle—K to last 3 sts, K 2 tog, K 1.

No. 3 needle—K 1, SKP, K to last 3 sts, K 2 tog, K 1.

Round 2—K all sts on all three needles.

Repeat these two rounds until there are 6 sts on No. 1 and No. 2 needles and 12 sts on No. 3 needle.

To Kitchener Stitch the Toe: Slip all sts on No. 1 and No. 2 needles onto one needle and break yarn, leaving about 18 inches. Thread this yarn into a tapestry needle. Hold the two needles together (parallel with each other) with the sts near the right end of needles. Insert needle, *knitwise,* into first st on the front needle and slip this st off. Insert needle *purlwise* into the second st on this same needle and pull the yarn through, leaving *this* st *on* the needle. *Then,* insert needle *purlwise* into first st on back needle and slip it off. Insert needle *knitwise* into the second st on same needle and pull yarn through, leaving *this* st *on* the needle. Continue in this manner until there is one st left on each needle. Pull out your knitting needles, run your hand up through the sock, and tack these 2 sts down to the sts right next to them. Weave thread into the seam made by decreasing, and cut off. Wash and block (see Tip 69).

ARGYLE SOCKS

MATERIALS
3-ply sock yarn
2 oz. Main Color—M
1 oz. of one Diamond Color—A
1 oz. of another Diamond Color—B
15 yds. of one Cross Color—C
15 yds. of another Cross Color—D
1 package of Yarn Bobbins
1 pr. SP Precision Tapered Knitting Needles, No. 2, Preferably 7-inch
1 set 7-inch DP Precision Tapered Knitting Needles, No. 2
GAUGE: $7\frac{1}{2}$ sts $=$ 1 inch

N.B. Before starting the ribbing of socks, wind two full bobbins each of the main color (M) and the two diamond colors (A and B)—also two bobbins each of the two cross colors (C and D). These do not need to be wound so full.

Argyle socks *must* be made on two needles, *working back and forth,* as long as there are changes of color being made.

Cast on 62 sts on the straight needles, with main color (M). Work in ribbing of K 2, P 2 for 3 inches (see Tip 35). Break yarn. The remainder of sock is worked in Stockinette Stitch.

On first row of pattern, following the chart, tie in your first bobbin of A. Leave about 3 inches of yarn when tying in. After first bobbin has been tied, and first 2 sts worked, tie in remaining eight bobbins (you will use only nine bobbins at any one time) when it comes their turn to be worked, as follows: Hold the new piece of yarn 3 inches from end and, using a crochet hook, insert it into back of the st *below* the next st on left-hand needle. Pull a loop of yarn through this bump, then pull the free end of yarn through the loop. This will tie the yarn in securely.

When changing one color for another, always put the yarn you have just finished using *over* the yarn you are going to use, bringing this new color up from underneath. This will avoid making a hole at the point of change of color.

When tying one color to another, after completion of diamonds, tie the two ends together with a square knot right up against the needle, leaving about three inches of free end, enough to thread a needle later on, to work into back when fastening off at end of work.

For Tall Diamond pattern, work according to Chart 1 (page 60).

For Flat Diamond pattern, work according to Chart 2 (page 61).

Heel. Slip off the first 16 sts onto one DP needle, 30 sts onto the second needle, and the last 16 sts onto the third needle. Turn the sts at end of third needle toward the sts at end of first needle, bringing the two outside edges of work together. Slip all 32 sts together on one needle. These make up the heel sts. The remaining 30 sts are to be worked in diamond pattern for the instep. Work on these sts, completing one, two, or three diamonds for the instep, keeping up the continuity of pattern, and before working the heel. Leave these sts on the needle. Break off all colors.

When heel has been completed and turned (see Plain Socks, page 56), using Main Color (M), break yarn and tie in at instep end of heel on the right side of heel, with right side of work facing you. Knit up sts from instep to heel (see Plain Socks), K off all sts on heel needle and K up same number of sts down the other side of heel toward instep, making the last st at the point of the instep. Purl back on all 54 sts. They will be rather crowded for the first few rows, but will ease up as work progresses.

To Decrease For Gusset:

Row 1—K 1, SKP, K to within last 3 sts of end of needle, K 2 tog, K 1.

Row 2—Purl all sts.

Repeat these two rows until 32 sts remain on needle.

Continue working in Stockinette St until side of gusset and foot measures same length as the instep piece, ending with a K row. Then, divide these 32 sts onto two needles (16 sts on each) numbering these needles No. 1 and No. 2, this designation to be used later. Join work, knitting every round, until sole of sock measures 1½ inches less than desired length.

To Toe off: Follow instructions for toe on plain socks (page 56).

To Finish: Graft gusset to instep (see Tip 68). Graft the back seam, using same color of grafting thread for the color of diamond.

DO NOT ATTEMPT TO PULL BACK AN ARGYLE SOCK BY REMOVING NEEDLES. Work it back to point of error, stitch for stitch. Watch carefully on every row to see that it is done correctly, checking with your chart, thus avoiding the necessity of pulling back more than one row.

If you will follow the Argyle chart faithfully, until you KNOW exactly what you are doing, you should have no ripping to do.

CHART 1, FOR TALL ARGYLE DIAMOND SOCKS

ROWS	(A)	(M	C	M	D	M)	(B)	(M	D	M	C	M)	(A)
1 & 2	2	13	1	0	1	13	2	13	1	0	1	13	2
3 & 4	3	11	1	2	1	11	4	11	1	2	1	11	3
5 & 6	4	9	1	4	1	9	6	9	1	4	1	9	4
7 & 8	5	7	1	6	1	7	8	7	1	6	1	7	5
9 & 10	6	6	1	8	1	5	10	5	1	8	1	5	6
11 & 12	7	3	1	10	1	3	12	3	1	10	1	3	7
13 & 14	8	1	1	12	1	1	14	1	1	12	1	1	8
15 & 16	8	0	1	14	1	0	14	0	1	14	1	0	8
	(A	C	A)	(M	(B	D	B	D	B)	(M)	(A	C	A)
17 & 18	7	1	2	12	2	1	12	1	2	12	2	1	7
19 & 20	6	1	4	10	4	1	10	1	4	10	4	1	6
21 & 22	5	1	6	8	6	1	8	1	6	8	6	1	5
23 & 24	4	1	8	6	8	1	6	1	8	6	8	1	4
25 & 26	3	1	10	4	10	1	4	1	10	4	10	1	3
27 &28	2	1	12	2	12	1	2	1	12	2	12	1	2
29 & 30	1	1	14	0	14	1	0	1	14	0	14	1	1

31 & 32	Same as Rows 28 & 27
33 & 34	" " " 26 & 25
35 & 36	" " " 24 & 23
37 & 38	" " " 22 & 21
39 & 40	" " " 20 & 19
41 & 42	" " " 18 & 17
43 & 44	" " " 16 & 15
45 & 46	" " " 14 & 13
47 & 48	" " " 12 & 11
49 & 50	" " " 10 & 9
51 & 52	" " " 8 & 7
53 & 54	" " " 6 & 5
55 & 56	" " " 4 & 3

Row 57 is worked the same as Row 2. Then, on Row 58, break off all A and B bobbins. Substitute B bobbins for A bobbins and substitute one A bobbin for the B bobbin. Then, work Row 3 with these same color changes. Keeping these color changes in mind, and substituting C for D and D for C, continue as follows

ROWS	(B)	(M	D	M	C	M)	(A)	(M	C	M	D	M)	(B)
59 & 60	3	11	1	2	1	11	4	11	1	2	1	11	3
61 & 62	4	9	1	4	1	9	6	9	1	4	1	9	4
63 & 64	5	7	1	6	1	7	8	7	1	6	1	7	5

ETC.

CHART 2, FOR FLAT ARGYLE DIAMOND SOCKS

ROWS	(A)	(M	C	M	D	M)	(B)	(M	D	M	C	M)	(A)
1	2	13	1	0	1	13	2	13	1	0	1	13	2
2	3	11	1	2	1	11	4	11	1	2	1	11	3
3	4	9	1	4	1	9	6	9	1	4	1	9	4
4	5	7	1	6	1	7	8	7	1	6	1	7	5
5	6	5	1	8	1	5	10	5	1	8	1	5	6
6	7	3	1	10	1	3	12	3	1	10	1	3	7
7	8	1	1	12	1	1	14	1	1	12	1	1	8
8	8	0	1	14	1	0	14	0	1	14	1	0	8
	(A	C	A)	(M)	(B	D	B	D	B)	(M)	(A	C	A)	
9	7	1	2	12	2	1	12	1	2	12	2	1	7
10	6	1	4	10	4	1	10	1	4	10	4	1	6
11	5	1	6	8	6	1	8	1	6	8	6	1	5
12	4	1	8	6	8	1	6	1	8	6	8	1	4
13	3	1	10	4	10	1	4	1	10	4	10	1	3
14	2	1	12	2	12	1	2	1	12	2	12	1	2
15	1	1	14	0	14	1	0	1	14	0	14	1	1

16	Same as Row 14
17	" " " 13
18	" " " 12
19	" " " 11
20	" " " 10
21	" " " 9
22	" " " 8
23	" " " 7
24	" " " 6
25	" " " 5
26	" " " 4
27	" " " 3
28	" " " 2
29	" " " 1

Break off A and B bobbins. Substitute B bobbins for A bobbins and an A bobbin for the B bobbin.

Substitute C bobbins for D bobbins and D bobbins for C bobbins, without breaking off the yarn, as these colors will cross at this point. Keeping these color changes in mind, continue as follows:

ROWS	(B)	(M	D	M	C	M)	(A)	(M	C	M	D	M)	(B)
30	2	13	1	0	1	13	2	13	1	0	1	13	2
31	3	11	1	2	1	11	4	11	1	2	1	11	3
32	4	9	1	4	1	9	6	9	1	4	1	9	4

ETC.

READER'S NOTES